FALMOUTH TO HELFORD

A view from the sea

by

Frank Pearce

DYLLANSOW TRURAN

I

Typesetting and Cover Design by: Delta Graphics, Unit 1, Intrepid Works,
Tregoniggie Industrial Estate, Falmouth, Cornwall (0326) 76044
Printed by: Earles Press, Station Hill, Redruth, Cornwall

ISBN No: 1 85022 007 7

FOREWORD

The object of this small book is to provide the reader who takes the boat trip from Falmouth, across the bay to the beautiful river Helford, with a deeper appreciation of its historical background and serve as a guide to the numerous points of interest. It does not claim to cover the history of the river in every detail, but if after the river trip, it encourages its readers to explore the countryside through which the Helford winds its way, then its object will have been achieved.

At the same time, it does claim to be a most useful handbook to point out the outstanding features in and around this magnificent waterway from the port of Falmouth to the snug little village of Gweek at the butt of the Helford River. The whole route is steeped in recorded history and nostalgic memoirs and the account produced here, is to the best of the author's knowledge from detailed research, a representation of the facts as they are known.

It is hoped that when the holiday is over, this souvenir digest will provide many hours of memorable interest and pleasure and stimulate the desire for a return visit to this pearl of the Cornish Riviera.

CONTENTS

	Page
Falmouth and the Killigrews	10
The Packet Ships and Piracy	13
The Customs House and Smuggling	18
Pendennis and St Mawes Castles	23
The Helford Estuary	29
The Church of St Anthony in Meneage	30
The Church of Manaccan	33
The Manacle Rocks and Wrecks	35
Wreck of the Bay of Panama	36
Helford Passage and Ferry Boat Inn	38
Porth Navas and Oyster Farm	41
The Fort at Dennis Head	42
Fishing Disputes in the Helford	43
Trelowarren Manor	45
The Church at St Mawgan	46
The Seal Sanctuary	47
Gweek	48

LIST OF ILLUSTRATIONS

	Page
Map of Falmouth	8 & 9
Falmouth Harbour and Docks	11
Cutty Sark at Falmouth c.1928	12
The King's Pipe — Falmouth	19
Falmouth from Flushing	22
Pendennis Castle	23
St Mawes Harbour	25
St Anthony Lighthouse and Old Sailing Ships	26
St Anthony in Meneage	30
Map of Helford River	31
Manaccan Church	33
Bay of Panama (wrecked at Nare Point)	36
Old Ferry Boat Inn — Helford Passage	38
Helford Passage and River	39
Shipwrights Arms — Helford Village	39
Helford Village	40

ACKNOWLEDGEMENTS

The author and publisher wish to express their sincere appreciation to Mr Hodges of the Porth Navas Oyster Farm and Mr B Denton for their kind help and co-operation towards the collection of information contained in this book.

V

ESTUARY

Vast sea I cannot stay your surging tidal flood
As past my ancient hills you pour your ocean blood
I watch in silence as your tide runs swiftly by
Regarding thus I wonder whence you come and why.

Thief-like you tread to search my every creek and bay
Quite unashamed your mighty power brooks no delay
But once within my gentle hills which ages span
Ere' man was new for I was here since time began
'Tis I who will direct your course and flow
And you must follow where I choose you go.

Fresh from the great Atlantic sea you search each creek
A bartering of nature silent and discreet
And deep within the folds of land each valley brings
From high a thousand rivulets of virgin springs.

And soon my babbling brooks descend to meet
Your saline blood to intercourse so brief and sweet
But soon the ageless voice of time you must obey
And then as gently as you came will steal away.

Frank Pearce.

INTRODUCTION

Running south from the Cornish mainland is a neck of land known as the Lizard peninsula. A land rich in historical association with smuggling and wrecking and steeped in drama and adventure of days long ago. Embraced within the valleys of this land flows a river, one of the most beautiful in the British Isles — The Helford.

From Falmouth Bay into which the Atlantic pours its ocean blood, a tidal flood glides with silent and almost imperceptible mobility. There among steep and gentle hills and richly wooded creeks it treads thief-like into every inlet and waterway. Largely unsullied by the ravages of modern progress, its beauty lies in the almost incomparable peace and tranquility of its still waters. From a thousand rivulets of virgin springs, tiny brooks babble their paths to small creeks bowered by venerable trees hallowed by age.

During the season, thousands of holiday makers visit this enchanting river in pleasure boats which ply between Falmouth and The Helford. To many, Helford River will immediately bring to mind the word association of 'Frenchman's Creek' known to every reader of Daphne Du Maurier's famous novel of the same name.

The historical and modern aspects of the trip from Falmouth can fairly be divided into three geographical areas of tidal water:

'Falmouth — Falmouth Bay — Helford River'

Even before the boat leaves Falmouth's Prince of Wales Pier one is assailed by the predominance of the port's fascinating association with the past. Here the beauty of the estuary, enhanced by long historical connections, echoes the activities of great sea captains and inglorious wreckers, noblemen and smugglers, kings and pirates.

To adequately assess the fascination of this geographical enrichment of the Cornish Riviera, one has to understand the drama and tradition of its evolution which inherently embraces the whole of the tidal way and its famous bay.

The popularity of Falmouth as a holiday resort has not only been maintained but largely increased by wise legislation refusing to allow it to become spoiled by modern progress with its fondness for converting seafronts into concrete jungles of artificial promenades and pseudo promontories.

7

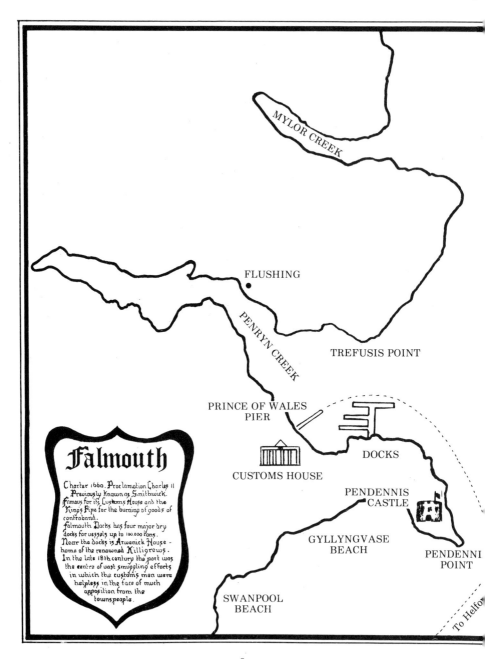

MYLOR CREEK

FLUSHING

PENRYN CREEK

TREFUSIS POINT

PRINCE OF WALES
PIER

DOCKS

CUSTOMS HOUSE

PENDENNIS
CASTLE

GYLLYNGVASE
BEACH

PENDENNI
POINT

SWANPOOL
BEACH

To Helfo

Falmouth

Charter 1660. Proclamation Charles II
Previously Known as Smithwick.
Famous for its Customs House and the
Kings Pipe for the burning of goods of
contraband.
Falmouth Docks has four major dry
docks for vessels up to 100.000 tons.
Near the docks is Arwenick House -
home of the renowned Killigrews.
In the late 18th century the port was
the centre of vast smuggling efforts
in which the customs men were
helpless in the face of much
opposition from the
townspeople.

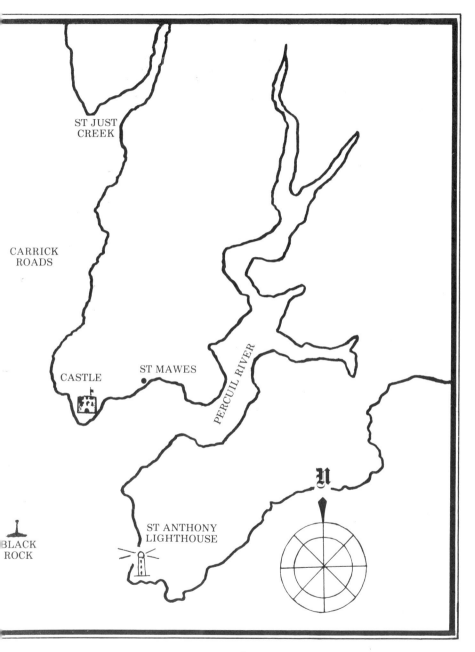

ST JUST
CREEK

CARRICK
ROADS

CASTLE

ST MAWES

PERCUIL RIVER

BLACK
ROCK

ST ANTHONY
LIGHTHOUSE

Falmouth and the Killigrews

Although the history of the town really begins with the date it received its Charter in 1660, records place it as far back as the early Celtic era. Prior to the grant of the Charter it was called Smithwick, reputedly derived from a St. Mithick and was situated on the south side of the creek near Market Strand. At that time it was merely a hamlet but as the years passed, the growing district adopted the new name of 'Pennycomequick', believed to have originated from the Celtic 'Pen-y-cum' — 'head of the vale'.

As early as 1613, one of the residents of Smithwick, Sir John Killigrew who lived at Arwenack House held the manor which included Pendennis Point. It was his efforts, allied to those of Sir Walter Raleigh, to improve the location and establish a township, which produced bitter objection from Penryn and Truro. The resentment felt by the people of Penryn in particular, led to a turbulent and bloody feud between the Killigrews and their close neighbours which lasted for years.

It was in the first year of the reign of Charles II that a Royal proclamation declared that the name of Falmouth should be adopted. The proclamation is an historic document and worth quoting:—

> Whereas our village of Smithwick, alias Pennycomequick is an ancient and popular village situate upon the sea-coast and near adjoining our port of Falmouth which is a most safe and capacious harbour for ships, insomuch that merchants and mariners, as well as natives and foreigners, have used to assemble from divers parts to the village and port aforesaid, with their ships, goods and merchandise, for the purpose of buying and selling the same freely from day to day etc., we will order and grant, that now and for ever hereafter, our village aforesaid, with the port aforesaid is and shall be one free village and that from henceforth it shall not be called, named or known by the name of the village Smithwick, but in all times hereafter shall be called, named or known by the name of our town of Falmouth

It was in the following years that the King gave the town its Charter of incorporation, no doubt in recognition of its great stand against the Parliamentary forces in 1646.

The Killigrews still maintained their dream of making Falmouth into a great port and in the year 1670, Sir Peter Killigrew constructed a quay with the result that maritime business greatly increased, bringing with it prosperity to the town.

As we move out into the inner harbour, Penryn creek lies away to the left with the village of Flushing on its right bank, the great wide waterway known as the Carrick Roads stretches ahead and the hills of St. Just in Roseland rise beyond. Further to the right, the harbour of St. Mawes nestles at the foot of the foreland guarding the entrance to the Percuil River.

The first feature on our immediate right is of course the huge area of Falmouth Docks structured from the initial effort of Sir Peter Killigrew, comprising four major dry docks. The largest was completed in 1953 and is capable of taking vessels of up to 100,000 tons. Although the foundation stone of the 'New Docks' was laid in 1860, the dry docks themselves had leisurely developed from 1820, an issue which showed a great deal of foresight for the future development of the town. Were it not for the fact that Falmouth had by then started to develop dry docks, Falmouth would have collapsed as a port. In building a dry dock capable of taking vessels of up to 100,000 tons it was felt at the time, that vessels of this weight would be the ultimate limit, as anything larger would break up in rough seas. When one considers that today, ships of 500,000 tons are in regular service, and that two of one million tons are on the drawing board, it makes you wonder if there are any limits to the size of maritime transport for the future.

Here within the inner harbour, one can see a fleet of small craft at their moorings and nearby a host of expensive cabin cruisers within the safe confines of the new Marina, but fifty years ago in these same waters were anchored old wooden-walled ships such as the famous old China tea-clipper 'Cutty Sark', then used as a training ship for boys.

The Pen Creek leads up to that very ancient borough which received its Charter way back in 1236 A.D. For most of its history it has been known as the 'Granite Town'. Its public buildings, shops, inns and houses are all constructed of that same material. Even London's famous Waterloo Bridge was built of Penryn granite. The town was a thriving little harbour some three to four hundred years before Falmouth came into existence. Its granite quay which still serves small craft, played a large part in the growth of the town, indulging in free trading with the many Spanish ships which sailed through the waters of the small creek.

Between the Killigrews of Arwenack House at Falmouth and the people of Penryn, the era of dissension grew into periods of hatred and conflict. In 1584 Dame Mary Killigrew commissioned a boatload of the locals to quietly board a Spanish merchant ship lying at anchor nearby, who then on her instructions proceeded to murder the crew and pillage the ship. Although she was condemned to death, she was later pardoned and 'sheltered by the people of Penryn'.

The Packet Ships and Piracy

As the years passed, further improvements in the landing stages and quays followed with the result that the year 1688 produced the 'golden age' of the town by the establishment of the post office 'Packet Station' — these famous vessels sailing to America, the West Indies and other foreign countries. Altogether about forty packet ships operated about one hundred voyages each year. These old sailing packets not only carried mail and parcels but were the only means of conveying money for business transactions. These gold carrying vessels were therefore the prey of marauding privateers along the coasts of France and America. Many were the stories of adventure involving these pirate ships often against overwhelming odds.

One typical example is the celebrated story of the formidable and courageous Captain Rogers, commanding a packet called the *Windsor Castle* which, in 1807 with a crew of only twenty eight and few guns, looked an easy prize to the heavily armed French pirate ship *La Jeune Richard* carrying a crew of 109 off Barbados.

Despite the odds, Captain Rogers successfully resisted the repeated attempts by the enemy to board his ship and in a most unusual but capable manner aimed his cannon, loaded to the muzzle with grape-shot and musket balls on to the intending boarders. The raking fire was devastating and this action was immediately followed by Captain Rogers and half-a-dozen of his men leaping aboard the enemy ship brandishing their cutlasses, driving the pirate crew below and allowing them to seize the vessel intact.

The following is taken from the *Royal Cornwall Gazette* dated 14th November 1807, quoting a letter from Captain Rogers which is conspicuous for its modesty, says little or nothing of the heroism displayed and is almost apologetic in character.

Captain Sutton of the *Windsor Castle* packet, having obtained permission to tarry at home while his ship performed its voyage to the West Indies, entrusted the command of her to Mr. William Rogers and later was surprised to receive the following letter from his worthy deputy, sent from Carlisle Bay — Barbados 4th Oct. 1807.

Dear Sir,

I am happy to inform you of our arrival at Barbados after 36 days passage. On the 1st Oct. last we fell in with the French privateer *La Jeune Richard*. After two hours action, she struck to the *Windsor Castle*. We had 13 killed and wounded. The privateer 57 killed and wounded. All the main mizzen and rigging is shot away as is the mainyard. If I can fish the mizzen mast and mainyard until I get to Antigua I will. All the mizzen and main channels are shot away by her long 24 pounder and our sails very much damaged. We have had great fatigue during these last four days, having only eleven men left to do the ship's duty and mount guard over 56 prisoners. When we took possession of her we found her decks covered with killed and wounded. We shall not be able to sail from this place for this week to come.

I am dear Sir, your humble servant,

William Rogers.

This is followed by another *Gazette* report dated 4th Aug. 1810.

Acting Captain James was with Captain Mudge when the *Queen Charlotte* was captured in 1805 and with Captain Bull when the *Duke of Marlborough* was taken in 1804.

A letter from William James to Christopher Saverland at Falmouth.

Sir,

At about one o'clock p.m. on 27th July, I espied a vessel to the E.S.E. standing to Southward which soon tacked to Northward, bore up and made sails to chase us. Upon which suspecting her to be an enemy, I caused the private signal to be made and cleared ship for action. At about a quarter before four, she hoisted French colours and was coming up very fast. I then cut away the jolly boat from the stern and made every preparation for the defence of the ship. At four, we commenced the action with our stern and quarter guns. About half past four, the privateer having the advantage in sailing was close alongside and attempted to board but was repulsed. We continued a close action, our yards being frequently locked in theirs until half past six, when we fortunately shot away her main top mast and soon after, she thought proper to haul to

14

Northward and stand away from us. From being so near I had an opportunity of seeing the enemy exactly. She was a French brig privateer mounting fourteen 18 pounders and two long forward guns and was full of men. It becomes my duty to report the great support I received from the Officers and the steady obedient and manly conduct of the crew.

Signed,

William James.

On the 14th April 1813 the American privateer *Annaconda* of 18 guns and 120 men captured the packet ship *Express*. After one and a half hours fight the rigging of the *Express* was cut to pieces and her hull damaged. The privateer took £10,000 and the spare rigging, sails etc — threw the guns overboard and gave back the ship.

Among the well known tombstones in nearby Mylor Churchyard is one bearing testimony to the gallant Captain Bull of the famous packet ship *Duke of Marlborough*. It appears that from the date of his commission as Captain of this packet ship in 1801 with the sincere intention of commanding a ship on purely peaceful missions of carrying mail and money to all parts of the world, he was for the next twelve or fourteen years frequently engaged in hand to hand fighting with pirate ships known as privateers. The following reports taken from newspapers of that period give some indication of the exciting trials and adventures to which he was subjected during this period of his life.

1804. July. The Packet ship *Duke of Marlborough* was captured when captained by Captain Bull on the 25th April by a French schooner of ten guns and one hundred men after one and a quarter hours and carried into Guadaloupe. The Packet carried six small connonades and 30 men. The ships were grappled together and the fighting was hand to hand, Captain Bull receiving a wound in the face. He, the Surgeon and two of the crew returned on the *Lady Arabella*, arriving on July 25th. They had been well treated on the privateer but were thrown into a dungeon at Guadaloupe. The Packet was then fitted up as a privateer with 20 guns and 160 men. There are sixty other privateers at present at Guadaloupe.

A year later in 1805 another *Duke of Marlborough* had been built at Falmouth with Captain John Bull being appointed to its command in January 1806, little knowing that he was soon to find himself once again the subject of a pirate ship's attention.

1808. Sailed Oct. 30th and reached Madiera on 10th November. Sailed for Rio on 12th Nov. On the 18th day at daylight between the Canary and Cape Verde Islands, fell in with the French brig corvette *La Josephine* of fourteen 24 pounders and 68 men, which chased and came up with the *Marlborough* and after a running fight of three hours, the Packet having received a dangerous shot between wind and water and otherwise much injured with no chance of escaping, Captain Bull was obliged to sink the mail and strike his colours. It did not suit the Frenchmen's purpose however to encumber himself with the prize, so after plundering her of her best sails and ropes, throwing her guns and some stores overboard and taking out six of her youngest men, the enemy left her. The mail having been sunk, Captain Bull returned to Falmouth.

1810. Oct. 5th. *The Marlborough* (Captain Bull) arrived on Monday eight days from Lisbon but having thrown her mail and dispatches overboard was in an engagement with a French privateer. The engagement took place off the Manacles (Lizard Peninsula) on Monday morning with a French schooner of 14 guns and full of men. Captain Bull defended his ship with usual bravery and the enemy did not fire until within half a pistol shot and commenced the action under a bloody flag meaning 'no surrender'.

It lasted about fifty minutes. She attempted to board the Packet but was received with well-directed fire which did great execution and drove the men from their quarters. Had there been a breeze there is little doubt that the Packet would have taken her, but profiting by the calm she got out her oars and rowed off. The schooner had scarcely left when an enemy cutter appeared and the Packet cleared for action a second time. Lieutenant Cock of the Lizard Signal Station had assembled some brave fellows and went to the assistance of the Packet but the cutter made off.

1810. Oct. 24th. The Falmouth Packet Mutiny.
When Custom's officers boarded the *Duke of Marlborough* as they were about to sail, they confiscated private items from the seamen's chests. Part of the crew mutinied and were pressed

into the Royal Navy, and the Packet sailed later with replacements from *H.M.S. Experiment*.

1814. April 2nd. The *Duke of Marlborough* packet ship on the outward voyage to Lisbon, fell in with a ship called *Primrose*, a sloop. Both vessels mistook each other for enemies, and two and a half hours of action took place before the error was discovered. A passenger Lieutenant Andrews was killed and several seamen injured. The passengers presented Captain Bull with a sword and a letter of praise and money for the crew in recognition of his gallant action. At a later naval Court Martial Captain Philpott of the *Primrose* was censured and no complaint made about Captain Bull.

1814. April 5th. Letter from passengers of *Duke of Marlborough* to Captain Bull re the action with *Primrose* — Admiration of your conduct and that of your gallant crew in the recent close action when a vessel three times the force, which would no doubt have terminated in destruction and capture if not recognised as the *Primrose*. Thank you for the kind and humane attention to passengers in particular the ladies.

Captain Bull was presented with a sword worth 250 dollars and 400 dollars to be divided among the crew.

1814. Nov. 22nd. The *Duke of Marlborough* was in action on the 19th with an American privateer schooner of 14 guns. The engagement lasted from daylight until 11 o'clock when the privateer stood off.

Captain Bull died on June 1st 1851 aged 80 and was buried at Mylor. Alas, the final chapter of the Golden Age of the Falmouth Packet ships came to an end about the year 1850 when by the introduction of the new steam ships and their shorter passage times and by the more rapid transit of passengers with the coming of the railway, the whole of the mail business was transferred to Southampton and Liverpool.

Courageously refusing to be daunted by the transfer of the 'Packet' trade to other ports, Falmouth set about developing the natural resources of its geographical position. The town ignored the smaller harbours tucked away in the Northern creeks and rapidy set to work to build the excellent harbour and dock facilities on its Southern banks, the foundation stone of which was laid in 1860.

The Customs House and Smuggling

The vast amount of shipping using the port of Falmouth in the 18th and 19th centuries more than justified the setting up of a Customs and Excise establishment within the precincts of the harbour. The first Customs House was built as early as 1652, before the town received its Charter even. A second was constructed in 1785 and the existing building in 1814. The present structure is a classic example of the elegant Georgian accommodation of the period, embracing the famous Long Room containing a fine old wall clock made by the Falmouth clockmaker J. Martin of about the same date. Over the portals of the pillared entrance there is a splendid Georgian Coat of Arms. In the lower part of the headquarters, one can still see the iron rings in the wall where the Preventive officers tethered their horses whilst reporting for duty.

At the rear of the building, facing the side road, is a well built chimney (known far and wide as 'The King's Pipe) in which contraband goods, seized from the smugglers, were burned from time to time. There seems to have been some doubt, whether the 'King's Pipe' ever consumed as much as it was intended it should as is revealed in an article from the *West Briton* newspaper dated 26th November 1815. Satirical and insinuative in character, it reflects the deep resentment and suspicion felt by many of the Falmouth residents that disposal of the seizures was being grossly abused by the Customs officials themselves.

The article is headed — 'The seizure of Lord Wellington's venison' — but the last two sentences particularly emphasize the conviction that all was not as it should have been.

> The Custom's officers are patterns of zeal and diligence. The indefatigable industry in which they exert themselves to receive a ready transmission of intelligence by the Packets is purely commendable. Fearful that the passage of these vessels may be protracted by their being overladen, they watch with lynx-eyed vigilance, lest an extra pair of shoes should be taken aboard by a seaman who may be desirous to avoid wet feet. Many curious anecdotes relative to their public spirited efforts are related by the inhabitants of Falmouth. As the venison may spoil before the Board of Customs can decide on this novel care, it is recommended that the whole revenue phalanx at Falmouth proclaim a feast and wash down the venison with wine of which there seems to be no scarcity among them. If the buck should

18

not be condemned, they can say they used it as a perishable article to prevent it being devoured by the rats that invest the stores. The vermin are particularly mischievous at Falmouth Custom House. We have heard of them devouring entire packages of jewellery and carrying off whole cheeses without leaving a vestige behind them.

One would have thought that the fully staffed Customs establishment in the port would have greatly influenced the smuggling activities that went on, but it appears that the amount of contraband that was brought ashore was out of all proportion to the quantity of goods seized. The volume of these goods increased as the surrounding districts participated with the people of the town openly indulging in the 'deals'.

Seemingly there were 'ways and means of dealing with the Custom-House officers'. Often the Customs men were helpless in the face of much opposition and few spirited attempts were made to break the contraband trade, the officers preferring to 'not see' what went on rather than to risk their own lives. In fact there were few who did not play some part. Even the Mayor of Falmouth, a certain Captain Isaac Cocart, was himself engaged in smuggling at one time or another and it is recorded that about the year 1740 he brought into the harbour a considerable cargo of tea and other contraband goods.

September 1762 saw the arrival of three East India ships from China, bringing thousands of pounds worth of silks, muslins and tea, being the private enterprise of the officers and men. From towns as far as Helston, Redruth, Camborne and Truro and the districts around, people poured into Falmouth, boarded the ships and purchased according to their means. Each day's trading was like a floating market day with the inevitable result that in the following weeks, itinerant salesmen peddled the rare goods up and down the Duchy, much to their advantage.

If the Customs Officers were having a hard time at Falmouth in the seizure of goods, their Revenue cutters were most successful with cruises along the coast as is shown by the following extracts from the *Royal Cornwall Gazette* of that period.

August 1st 1801. Arrived the revenue cutter *Active* bringing with her the captured smuggling lugger *Morgan Rattler* belonging to Polperro laden with 644 casks of spirits.

May 8th 1802. Arrived the revenue cutter *Hind* bringing with her the captured smuggling vessel *Flora* laden with 822 casks of spirits.

May 12th 1802. Arrived the revenue cutter *Hind* bringing with her the captured smuggling vessel *Pearl* laden with spirits and tobacco.

In August 1802 there was a sale of condemned spirits at the Customs House at Falmouth, where brandy averaged eight shillings and fourpence per gallon and gin seven shillings and sixpence per gallon. The frustration and hostility towards the Customs Officers who tried to carry out their duties, is illustrated by a threatening letter received by one of the officials named Joseph Platt of the Falmouth service. A reward of £20 was offered by the Commissioners of Customs for any information leading to the arrest of the writer.

Pray to God to forgive you Joseph Platt, your doom is fixed — as Percival received his death by a ball so shall you fall. Your late proceedings with the Packets has driven me to despair and ere I leave this earth, my determination is fixed to put an end to your cruel and wicked existence unless you discontinue your committing such robbery as you and your brood have perpetrated for this some time past. I give you Joseph Platt to consider this as above until the 30th March 1813. My doctor friend although my cruel enemy and my ruin for the sake of your soul pray to Jesus to forgive you. I say again your fate is fixed.

Signed . . . . A friend to the community

Emerging into the great expanse of water known as the Carrick Roads, an area of some five square miles, we might well see busy tugs, pulling and pushing large tankers or cargo vessels into position to enter the docks for maintenance or repairs.

Across the river is the little village of Flushing and nearby the quay and docks of Little Falmouth where several of the Falmouth Packet ships were built and where the shipwrights employed in the work and their families settled. It is supposed to be one of the warmest places in Britain and was founded by the Dutch and named in memory of the larger Flushing in Holland.

The jutting headland nearby is Trefusis Point where in springtime the wooded slopes are carpeted with primroses and bluebells. It seems difficult to imagine that between the years 1840 to 1940 nine ships were blown on to this shoreline and wrecked with enormous loss of life. They still lie buried beneath the waters of this seemingly sheltered waterway.

Pendennis and St Mawes Castles

As we approach the mouth of the estuary our attention will be centred on the two old Castles, one on either side. It was Henry VIII who on fearing an invasion of Britain built the Castles — Pendennis on the conspicuous promontory commanding the Western entrance to the harbour and well elevated to dominate any attempt at infiltration by intruders, and St Mawes on the Eastern side to complete the control of all shipping entering or leaving the port. Both these Castles were completed in about 1543. They were built not for the defence of Falmouth as one would imagine (for at that time Falmouth did not exist) but for the defence and protection of Penryn against the marauding French, who never actually dared to run the gauntlet of fire which could have been produced between the two Castles overlooking the mouth of the estuary.

Between 1567 and 1643 various governors were appointed to the Castle of Pendennis, among whom were the Killigrews and the Parkers. By 1644 one of the most famous of them all, John Arundel, was aptly nicknamed 'John for the King'.

By the early 1620's, however, the Castles had fallen into a state of disrepair and in 1627 Sir Robert Killigrew, Captain of Pendennis Castle, informed the Council in London that he had dispatched 60 petitions in the last ten years for supplies, with the pay of his men

over a year in arrears; no guns were mounted and but three barrels of powder in store. Although a grant of over £1000 was made for repairs to Pendennis Castle the work was still not completed by 1642. Similar conditions prevailed at the St Mawes Castle — platforms were decayed, guns inoperative and no powder or ammunition was available.

Early in 1646, the Castle was besieged by land and sea by Parliamentary forces commanded by Colonel Fortescue and Admiral Batten under the Generalship of Sir Thomas Fairfax. Despite his eighty years, the Castle was stubbornly defended by John Arundel who refused all demands to surrender. Even with sufficient food left for only twenty four hours, the old man argued the terms of the treaty of surrender with such firmness that the besiegers never suspected the critical situation inside the Castle after its six months of siege and granted terms as good as to any other garrison in Britain.

On the water's edge, beneath the Castle is a large cave of about 100 feet long believed to have a small passage leading up to the Castle itself. One wonders just how many eminent and distinguished noblemen and even fleeing Royalty used this passage to escape their pursuers.

It was from here on July 14th 1644 that Queen Henrietta embarked for France after fleeing from Cromwell's soldiers and that two years later, the Queen's son the young Prince of Wales (later Charles II) found refuge in Pendennis Castle before escaping to the Isles of Scilly.

Across the mouth of the harbour its sister Castle St Mawes fared much worse against the Parliamentary forces and early in March 1646 the invading army arrived before St Mawes. Owing to its position on the slope of the hill, the Castle was almost impossible to defend against attack from the landward side and after a brief discussion on terms of capitulation between the Governor, Hannibal Bonython, and General Fairfax, the surrender took place on March 12th, a few days later.

St Mawes too, has had an eventful history, mainly in the area of smuggling which resulted in persistent battles of cunning and strategy between the Customs on the one hand and the contraband runners on the other, lasting over many years. It was there in the St Mawes river that the notorious smuggler and pirate, Robin Long operated, until he was caught red-handed in a bold and spirited adventure in the 17th century and eventually hanged in chains on a gibbet at a place called Ruan Lanihorne some distance inland.

Beyond St Mawes' wide entrance, looking Southward is the brilliant white pillar of St Anthony Lighthouse, 60 feet high above low water; its whiteness contrasting sharply against the mass of black rocks of the headland behind it. A central red beam shows in a Southerly direction, covering the dreaded Manacle Rocks just off the Lizard Peninsula with a white beam either side of the red; that on the left coming in from the sea giving clearance for entrance to Falmouth harbour and the one on the right giving clearance for coastal passage. The white light to the East has a range of thirteen miles.

In the middle of the estuary between St Anthony Head and Pendennis Point is the familiar Black Rock; the only hazard to shipping entering and leaving harbour but well-identified by the huge black granite cone mounted by a ball on a vertical iron standard.

Tradition has it that on this rock the Phoenicians bartered for Cornish tin. For many years the Killigrew family were responsible for keeping a tall pole fixed on this rock, which is covered at high tide, but later this duty was passed to the parish church which received one shilling from every ship entering the port to pay the cost of its upkeep. In 1835, Trinity House put the granite cone on the rock and set up the present standard.

As we survey the wide expanse of the Carrick Roads from its Northern locality of Trefusis Point to just Southward of St Anthony Head and Pendennis Point, it seems difficult to accept the fact that the wrecks of some fifty ships lie beneath these waters. Between the years 1720 and the early 1900's, the tempestuous South-Easterly gales claimed the lives of many hundreds of passengers and crew. The most incredible wrecks were probably the sinking of six German U. boats driven on to the rocks under the Castle Drive in 1921 where they remained for many years.

And so we enter Falmouth Bay, one of the finest harbours in the world, and head South-West toward the Eastern seaboard of the Lizard Peninsula.

On the right at Pendennis Point is the modern Coastguard Station now the district headquarters for all South West Cornwall, and opened by Prince Charles in 1981. Its powerful receiving and transmitting equipment covers the area from the river Camel on the North coast to Dodman Point in the South and extends a thousand miles out into the Atlantic Ocean. Manned 24 hours a day it is the co-ordinating centre for the rescue of ships in distress.

Among the merchant ships anchored in the bay there may well be a few Russian and Bulgarian factory ships. Cornish fishermen and others sell their catches of mackerel direct to these ships which process the fish on arrival. The foreign crews frequently visit Falmouth to buy what are to them luxury goods unobtainable in their own countries.

Towards the Southern horizon, one may well see a variety of merchant ships voyaging Eastwards or Westwards along the channel sea lanes. These may be giant tankers laden with oil from ports of the Red Sea, mammoth container ships from Japan and America or British coasters large and small, old and new ferrying their merchandise from one harbour to another, moving slowly but inexorably towards their ports of call.

A familiar sight over the bay are low flying helicopters from the Royal Navy's Air Station at Culdrose only a few miles from the Helford river. Apart from daily training flights of smaller helicopters, squadrons of large Sea Kings operate their Search and Rescue enterprises. These hazardous missions which are often carried out in the most atrocious weather conditions have been the means of saving hundreds of lives.

On our right, the long stretch of sandy beach known as Gyllyngvase is marked by its long natural esplanade and numerous hotels. The abundance of dracaenas (palm trees) in its attractive winter gardens is an indication of the warm climate enjoyed here.

Its fine seafront, bordered by an unspoilt promenade, is a feature which any resort would be proud to possess and when to this are added its public gardens and covered shrubberies, grottoes infused with types of tropical vegetation, a concert pavilion and the magnificent Castle Drive, one can begin to understand the reputation it has achieved from the discerning holidaymaker.

Adjacent to Gyllyngvase is Swanpool Beach highly popular with tourists. Lying close behind it is Swan Pool, a large fresh water lake about half-a-mile long, once owned by the Killigrew family and maintained as a breeding area for many swans. It is now used as a boating lake and is popular with model boat enthusiasts.

Between Swanpool and its neighbouring Mean Porth beach in 1865, over a thousand Roman coins, some dating back to the time of Constantine A.D. 306 were unearthed by farm workers while ploughing at Pennance Farm.

The next headland on the right is Rosemullion Head, which in common with many other coastal areas in Cornwall is owned by the National Trust.

The Helford Estuary

We are now at the mouth of the Helford River with Toll Point on the right and Dennis Head to the left, standing like gate posts between river and sea. Parson's Beach precedes Toll Point and above it, overlooking the estuary, is Mawnan church which like many others along the margins of the river, is very old with most interesting records. The church was originally dedicated to St Maunanus believed to have been a Breton monk who landed here in 520 A.D.

The earliest cruciform building appears to have been erected in the 13th century. Recently some interesting documents came to light among them an 'Account Book of the Overseers of the Poor' which gave details of certain funeral expenses. The items make interesting reading . . . . . .

Burial of Julian Woolcock

		£.s.d.
1722	Pd for a shroud and making for Julian Woolcock.	4—6
	Pd Bol Bab for shrouding and washing of corps.	3—6
	Pd John Thomas for Coffing.	9—0
	Pd for tobacco and pipes and candle lights.	1—0
	Pd more for Bread & Beer for ye time of watching.	1—7
	Pd for Beer and Brandy at Burial.	7—3
	Pd Henry Bab for making of Grave.	1—6
	Pd for buriing Julian Woolcock.	1—5—0

Burial of William Downing

1773	To Coffing for William Downing.	10—0
	To stripping and certificate.	5—6
	To 3 gallons Cider & 2 quarts of Spirits.	4—6
	To tea, sugar, bread, butter, candles, pipes, tobacco and watching.	2—6
	To shroud 2/11. Parson, clerk and sexton 5/—.	7—11
	To a hundred faggots and carriage.	6—6

Comment on the expenditure of intoxicating liquor for the funerals of Woolcock and Downing is superfluous.

By a minute of Parish Officers in 1849 it was resolved to offer the following wages to men out of work on the roads.

One man . . . . Three days at 10 pence per day.

One man . . . . Two days at 6 pence per day.

The Church of St Anthony in Meneage

Hidden among the trees on Dennis Head is the church of St Anthony in Meneage; the interpretation of Meneage being 'Land of the Monks'. Christian preaching was brought to Cornwall 1400 years ago by men and women who settled in hermitages, sometimes under the protection of friendly chiefs who founded 'Lans' or monastries.

The mellow grey stone church of St Anthony is admirably situated on the bank of a little inlet known as Gillan Creek.

Tradition has it that the church was built by a band of shipwrecked Normans who were caught in a storm while crossing from France to Britain and driven ashore near Gillan Creek. They had vowed that if saved they would build a church to St Anthony. Some credulity is given to this tradition by the fact that the tower is built of a fine grained granite of a kind unknown in Cornwall but which is found in Normandy.

Nearby can be seen ancient entrenchments of Celtic origin which were used again during the Civil War by the Royalists for the security of Helford harbour. They were surrendered by the Royalist

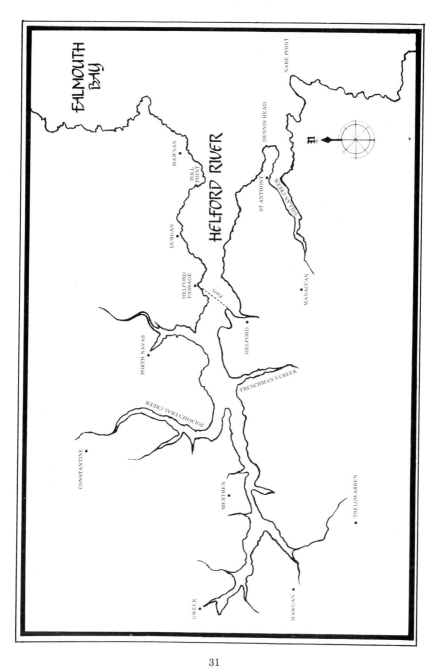

FALMOUTH BAY

MAWNAN •

TOLL POINT •

DURGAN •

HELFORD RIVER

HELFORD PASSAGE

Ferry

PORTH NAVAS •

HELFORD •

ST ANTHONY •

DENNIS HEAD

GILLAN CREEK

NARE POINT

MANACCAN •

FRENCHMAN'S CREEK

POLWHEVERAL CREEK

CONSTANTINE •

MERTHEN •

TRELOWARREN •

GWEEK •

MAWGAN •

31

Richard Vyvyan of Trelowarren to Sir Thomas Fairfax in March 1646 being the last place to hold out except for St Michael's Mount and Pendennis Castle.

Kingdom's Weekly Intelligence dated 17th March 1646 reported: 'St. Dennis Fort at Helford with 26 pieces of ordnance is surrendered.'

The church is very old, for a document dated 1170 A.D. mentions the church of St Antoninus an Egyptian Saint who was claimed as the patron saint of St Anthony in Meneage. Among the many interesting features is a beautiful wood carving of the Last Supper in the niche of the East wall believed to be 15th century German work. Here also are twenty lovely brass candelabra hanging from the roof, beautifully designed, which were presented by Professor Gleadowe who towards the latter end of his life came to live in the area. One of his best known works during his lifetime was the design of the Stalingrad sword presented to Russia at the end of World War Two.

On the boundary of the churchyard are the remains of an old 'whipping post' used at a time when each community applied its own punishment. One of the foundation stones of the tower is a huge slab of elvan to which the village stocks were formerly attached but although the chain still hangs nearby, the stocks themselves were removed to the neighbouring hamlet of Bosahan for preservation.

The Church of Manaccan

Not far away is the ancient 12th century Norman church of Manaccan. Perhaps the most gifted of all the vicars of Manaccan was Richard Polwhele (1794 — 1822) one of whose sons Edward fought under Nelson at Trafalgar. Mr Polwhele had an extensive circle of correspondents among whom were Sir Walter Scott and Captain Bligh (Bligh of the Bounty).

He made the acquaintance of the latter in a rather amusing way. During the Napoleonic War, Bligh was engaged in survey work on the Helford River when he was mistaken for a French spy and arrested. The vicar who was also the Justice of the Peace was having tea when the prisoner was brought in and not wishing to be disturbed ordered Bligh to be cast into the local lock-up, the vicarage coal cellar. Later in the charge room, Bligh made himself and his anger known. However, under Polwhele's consoling influence his anger subsided and after a hearty supper they parted on the best of terms.

It seems that Richard Polwhele was fond of a good wine cellar. Records prove that he had paid his predecessor £20 for the contents some of which were very good while some tasted strongly of salt water — evidence indeed that the barrels had been floated ashore by smugglers and delivered as 'Brandy for the Parson'.

The Fig Tree

One of the unusual features of the church is a great and ancient fig tree growing out of the South West wall. Its origin is unknown but it is established that the tree has been growing there for the last 200 years.

Manaccanite

The village itself has a mineralogical history for in 1692, the Reverend Gregor, who apart from his religious learning was also an expert in the scientific field, discovered a darkish sand in nearby rocks which at the time he assumed was gunpowder. On examination, the grains proved to contain among other ingredients, oxide of iron. The mineral is now known as Manaccanite. Fortunately for Manaccan, the deposits were never exploited, for far greater amounts were found in other parts of the world and became known as Titanium used as an alloy to toughen steel.

The Manacle Rocks and Wrecks

Before we enter the mouth of the Helford River and leave the great expanse of Falmouth Bay, our attention will be drawn to a projection of rocks to the South standing about a mile off shore near Porthoustock. These are the notorious Manacles, a semi-circular reef of visible and submerged rocks, the graveyard of many a fine sailing ship. The church of St Keverne a mile inland has such a close and tragic association with the Manacles that one cannot ignore its presence.

The churchyard holds the remains of some four hundred people who over the years have been drowned by shipwreck on this perilous part of the coast. The memorials within the church are almost wholly dedicated to the victims of shipwrecks. One window is in memory of a tragic night in October 1898 when the 7000 ton liner *Mohegan* struck the Manacles and sank in a few minutes drowning 106 of her passengers and crew who were later buried in the churchyard. Another monument is a memorial to two other ships driven ashore here in 1809 within hours of each other from which nearly 200 people lost their lives.

This however is only a part of the long tragic story for since the 18th century, almost 100 ships have foundered on these murderous rocks. The drama of the ocean has indeed cast its shadow over the peninsula.

Wreck of the Bay of Panama

A little to the South of Dennis Head and St Anthony Church is Nare Point. Here occurred one of the most tragic stories of shipwreck in Cornish history. In 1891, the four masted square-rigged ship *Bay of Panama* carrying a cargo of jute from Calcutta arrived off the Lizard coinciding with the great blizzard of '91, the worst weather the Duchy had known for over 200 years when sheep and cattle died in the fields in their hundreds.

On the morning of the 10th March, an enormous wave struck the vessel, carrying away all the deck boats. Minutes later she crashed into the cliffs at Nare Point and soon after another great wave hit the ship taking the Captain, his wife and seven of the crew. Some of the remainder of the crew found refuge in the rigging but, subjected to such cold and exposure, six seamen froze to death entwined in the mainstays while others, unable to maintain their grip, fell into the sea.

By daybreak the ship was fast under the cliff with her bow less than fifty feet away from the rocks. A farmer walking along the cliff was the first to spot the wreck and rushed to Porthallow to inform the coastguards who hurried to the wreck from St Keverne with rocket apparatus and having rigged a breeches buoy, brought ashore those that remained alive. Only seventeen men were saved out of the crew of forty and these with limbs frozen in the position in which they had clung to the rigging were then taken to St Keverne for the night where they were thawed out and fed.

But this was not the end of the story. The next day, a horse-drawn vehicle took them to Gweek at the head of the Helford river on their way to Falmouth but here huge snowdrifts blocked the road and they were forced to walk or stay and freeze to death. Thus in twenty four hours they had twice been subjected to the rigours of Arctic conditions and now had to battle their way through deep snow to eventually reach the outskirts of Falmouth some six miles distant.

The story of this nightmare experience brought sightseers from all over the South-West to view the wreck. Pieces of deck timber were cut and sold as souvenirs and the ship's bell given to a small mission chapel at Helford. Here in a small pinnacled tower it can be seen to this day, weather-beaten and green.

On the right we now pass the wooded valley of Carwinnion running to the sea and beside it the little waterside titheing of Durgan where a few years ago some of the film sequences of 'Treasure Island' were enacted. Behind, on higher ground, is the attractive valley garden of Glendurgan where among the labyrinth of laurels is a splendid Camellia Walk interspersed with rare shrubs and flora. The garden was cultivated by the late Alfred Fox and given in 1961 to the National Trust allowing the public to enjoy its landscaped beauty.

Helford Passage and Ferry Boat Inn

Within a few hundred yards the river narrows a little and we come to the Helford Passage with its famous inn. There has been an inn here since the 16th century when the river was a means of transport between Falmouth, Penzance and Newlyn. In the mid-1930's it was partly rebuilt but although of a fairly modern structure, the interior has been retained as far as possible and decorated in the image of its nautical concept with the walls bearing photographs of the original building. The atmosphere of the sea is reflected in old ships' lanterns which adorn the walls while the two bars designed and built by local craftsmen, bear evidence to its sea-faring association.

During the last war, the inn was adopted by American officers while they were based in Britain immediately in advance of the D-day operations. At that time Durgan woods contained scores of Nissen huts providing accommodation for American troops. Most of the concrete roads around the area built by the U.S. Forces allowed heavy tanks to reach Trebah beach from where they were loaded on to landing barges ready for the invasion of Normandy. It was from here also that huge sections of the famous Mulberry Harbour used off the beaches of France were shipped.

Nearby at the tiny Bar Beach, the local tradition of Trigging (or Cockle Gathering) on Good Fridays is upheld when scores of people arrive armed with buckets and hoes to collect the best cockles for the table.

Across the water on the opposite bank to the Ferry Boat Inn is the Club House of the Helford River Sailing Club from where each year two special races are organised to the Continent, a distance of about 100 miles, against Breton and French competitors who arrive from St Malo and Brest. The Spring Bank Holiday race terminates on the Saturday at L'Aberwrach Lifeboat Station where the yachtsmen are welcomed by the local Mayor. On August Bank Holiday weekend there is a similiar race to Camaret near Brest. One of the most popular events of the year is the night race in July from the Helford, around the Eddystone Lighthouse and back to Fowey.

We are now passing the pretty little village of Helford itself creeked into the left bank where, in a beautiful setting, thatched cottages retain the gracious charm of a bygone age. Here the little tributary leading to the village is spanned by a quaint wooden bridge.

Porth Navas and Oyster Farm

On the right, the entrance to Porth Navas Creek, known as Abraham's Bosom, comes into view. It is here at Porth Navas that the Duchy Oyster farm is now owned and operated by Mr Hodges who had previously managed the farm following the family tradition of several generations. In 1983, the oyster production was almost brought to a standstill by an unfortunate infiltration of a French oyster disease known as Bonamia. Mr Hodges is now engaged in a courageous fight to clean the oyster beds and restore the farm to its former successful cultivation.

Oysters are among the most extensively eaten of all sea-foods and the industry as a whole is one of the most valuable of those that utilize the products of river and sea. It has been under culture longer than any other water creature. Artificial cultivation flourished in China at a very remote period and there is ample evidence showing that in Italy culture began in about 100 B.C. Supplied from hatcheries, the oysters are re-laid on the river bed to reach maturity after about four years and when ready for marketing they are cleaned and purified before being dispatched to all parts of the country.

On the right we are now passing the oak woods of Calamansack, which with its ancient spelling of Kylmoncote recorded in 1249, is perhaps translated from our Cornish language as 'The Retreat on the Hillock'.

Now opposite, on the left bank is one of the river's most famous creeks — Frenchman's Creek — immortalised by Daphne du Maurier's novel of that name. It was near this creek in the early 1900's that timber from Norway was unloaded and floated to the village of Gweek at the head of the river. On the right is the richly wooded arm of Groyne Point where the river divides — the right tributary going to Polwheveral, a tiny hamlet which marks the end of the tidal flow, and the other to Gweek past Tremayne Quay and Merthen Woods. It was here in Merthen Woods during the mid-1960's that the Queen and Prince Philip picnicked at the old oyster house. The creek to Polwheveral is a narrow waterway extending almost up to Constantine, a sizeable village of about 2000 people that commands a beautiful view to the South across the creeks of Helford River.

Constantine Church is a spacious building of local granite dating back to the second half of the 15th century containing features of historical interest and it is generally supposed that the patron saint who gave his name to Constantine was king of Dumnonig (Cornwall and Devon) during the 5th century who, repenting of his crimes, retired to a monastery and lived the rest of his life in saintly devotion.

During the 16th century, the river, like its creeks and neighbouring hamlets came under the influence of the Killigrews of Arwenack. Sir John Killigrew at the close of the century was accused before the Privy Council of warning a noted pirate named Elliott whilst he was anchored in the Helford river that His Majesty's vessel *Crane* was coming to arrest him. It seems that Killigrew provided Elliott with certain provisions and received in return a substantial bribe enabling the pirate to escape his pursuers. Not long after this episode, Elliott fled to Spain and allied himself to the Spanish war service. Following this it was reported by spies of the English who were in Spain that rumour had it in that country that Killigrew himself was in league with the Spaniards to surrender Pendennis. But as the years passed, the danger of Spanish invasion gradually melted away.

The Fort at Dennis Head

The English became embroiled in their own Civil War of the 1640's but the area of the Helford remained largely undisturbed with the same families continuing to rule the parishes throughout the reign of Charles I and the Restoration. During the war the area was controlled by the Royalist strongholds at Pendennis and Dennis Head. Forced levies of men and money were made for their defences, but the fort on Dennis Head was rebuilt and garrisoned mainly at the expense of Sir Richard Vyvyan of nearby Trelowarren who owned the land and waterage bordering the river at Merthen and Calamansack. The area remained calm enough for the next three years but as already mentioned, suddenly in March 1646, the fort was surrounded by Parliamentary forces and compelled to surrender to Sir Thomas Fairfax.

Fishing Disputes in the Helford

There was constant bitter wrangling during the next 200 years over the fishing and oyster rights of the river. Most Cornish rivers were under the control of some manor or other, and from a very early date the Lord of Merthen claimed jurisdiction over the higher creeks and waters of the Helford River from the Passage up to Gweek. Additionally an ancient document declared:—

> There has been a certain custom within the Manor of Merthen from a time beyond the memory of man, that the Lord of the Manor shall have the best fish called Porpos and Dolphyn and all other such great fishes in whatsoever place caught between the Passage and Gweke . . . . and that all fish of this sort shall be brought to Groyne Point and then divided.

However, as time passed, landowners who lived by the river-side claimed the right of free-fishing — accepting the overlordship of the Lord of the Manor though challenging his rights and privileges by open fishing in the preserved waters.

In 1659 however, Sir Richard Vyvyan addressed a Bill of Complaint to the Court of Chancery because he claimed his rights had been infringed by fishermen living on the shores of the river. He showed that he was Lord of the Manor of Merthyn upon the navigable river of Helford and that all his predecessors had enjoyed certain ancient liberties and privileges over the river from the Passage up to Gweek Bridge and throughout the creeks between these places. In these creeks it was not lawful for anyone to hunt, hawk, fowl, fish or dredge for oysters without license from the lords of the manor, who moreover, were entitled to the chief or best fish, likewise to all wrecks found above the Passage. Furthermore, that all those kind of fish so taken were to be parted and divided at Merthen Green and not elsewhere, so that the lord or his deputy might there choose the head or best fish before such division; but the lords of Merthen were entitled to the benefit of anchorage, keelage and bushellage due for all vessels anchoring or unlading in any of the creeks. In spite of this however, Samuel Haydon of Mawgan, John Cockram of Manaccan and Thomas Lugge with several others occupying lands on the shores of the Helford River, had most unjustly violated these privileges, had fowled, fished, dredged for oysters, set nets, refused to give up the head fishes, anchored their boats, barges and other vessels and unladed them without paying any dues. Sir Richard besought the Court of Chancery to appoint a Commission to sit locally and hear the evidence of the witnesses.

As a result, a Commission was appointed to take the depositions. They sat at Penryn on March 30th 1659. Only the evidence given by the supporters of the defendant is preserved and is of a very non-commital character. Sir Richard however, was able to produce some convincing arguments in the shape of certificates signed by local men during the years preceding the trial, who in the presence of witnesses had sought leave of Sir Richard to set nets in the river, thereby acknowledging the right and royalty of the river to belong to Sir Richard as owner of Merthen.

One of the witnesses John Mayne also attested that he had seen one Baldman, son in law of Sampson Cockram of Helford, pull down the stone called Mayne Brough in order to obliterate Sir Richard's boundary mark. Such evidence, albeit written by Sir Richard and signed with the marks and signatures of witnesses, and overawed no doubt by the splendours of Trelowarren and the fiery temper of the old Cavalier, seem to have carried the day for Sir Richard. So for a time, the rights and privileges of the lord of the manor was upheld by the law. But in the mid-1880's, a determined effort was made by the fishermen to assert what they conceived to be their rights. This led in 1847 to an action for trespass brought by the lessees of the oyster grounds against a number of local men. The defence was that the river was open to public navigation and that when the inhabitants ventured to dredge for oysters, the plaintiff first tried to stop them by procuring an armed cutter from the Admiral at Plymouth. The officer in charge refused however to stop any persons from dredging for oysters declaring that he was only there to prevent violence. The plaintiff however, took matters into his own hands. He could not secure the lower part of the river, so to keep the upper part inviolate, he moored a row of boats across the river to mark its limits and assembled a large body of miners from the mine at Constantine armed with sticks and bludgeons for its defence.

However, some of the conditions of the leases were still strictly adhered to right up to the 20th century, for as late as the 1930's, within the living memory of the Hodges family, an amount of 240 oysters had to be delivered to the Vyvyan manor every week.

Trelowarren Manor

We are now in the higher reaches of the river where, on the left, Bishop's Quay flanks Mawgan Creek and the tributary runs to within a short distance of the Trelowarren estate and the village of Mawgan.

Trelowarren Manor is listed in the Doomsday Survey but there is no record of the exact position of the old house or of the Priory which is said to have existed there up to the 14th century.

Two families known to have lived there in the 13th and 14th centuries were Cardinan and Ferrers, both now extinct. In the year 1427, John Vyvyan of Trevidren in the parish of St Buryan married Honor Ferrers of Trelowarren and the present family are descended from that marriage. Up to the time of the marriage into the Ferrers family many of the Vyvyans appear to have been of a lawless nature and several were excommunicated for assault and, possibly, robbery on the highways. Several Vyvyans were appointed Captains of St Mawes Castle, starting with Michael in 1544 when the Castle was approaching completion. The most famous was probably Hannibal whose son Francis was also made Captain of St Mawes and later became involved in proceedings in the Star Chamber where he was fined £2000 for drawing money for men to man the Castle who did not exist. But as other Vyvyans were subsequently made Captains, this smear on the family history does not seem to have been sustained. The first of the Vyvyans to become a Baronet was Sir Richard Vyvyan who was made Master of the Mint to Charles I in the Civil War, the honour being conferred on him in September 1644.

The Church at St Mawgan

Not far from the head of the creek lies the delightful little village of Mawgan. Its church has the remains of a chancel and nave dating back to the 13th century but it is probable that the earliest church on this site was built in the 6th century.

Although restored as late as 1895, many interesting features are of 13th and 16th century vintage.

The South aisle is by tradition known as the Carminow Aisle on account of its two life-sized effigies in freestone which lie in a wall recess under the window. These represent a Crusader in the reign of Edward I, Sir Roger Carminow who died in 1308 and the Lady Johanna his wife. They are thought to have been brought here in the reign of James I, from the now non-existent chapel of Carminow.

Fixed high on a pillar near the pulpit is an interesting little brass. It has an inscribed skull and cross-bones and a four-line acrostic of the words 'Shall we all dye', which goes as follows:—

'Hannibal Basset here interred doth lye,
Who dying lives to all Eternitye,
Hee departed this life the 17th Jan 1708,
In the 22nd year of his age — a lover of learning.'

'Shall wee all dye,
wee Shall dye all,
all dye Shall wee,
dye all wee Shall.'

Just below the church is the old *Ship Inn*, renowned for its story of the three notorious highwaymen — Barnicoat, Lillicoat and Dawe — who terrorised the neighbourhood around the nearby Goonhilly Downs. Operations were directed against unprotected wayfarers who ventured along this lonely stretch of moorland. The farming community was particularly vulnerable to their activities. Farmers and drovers who took their cattle to the inland market town for sale and returned at night with the proceeds would be fair game and 'ripe for the plucking'. At length their luck ran out as they were caught and brought before the local judge Sir Courtenay Vyvyan at Mawgan and sentenced in this pub. The actual courtroom still exists.

In the centre of the village, on a small triangular piece of grass, stands a tall stone some seven feet high which makes the history of the church modern by comparison. Shapeless, green with lichen, eroded in weather, it appears at first to have no special significance but on close examination there are traces of lettering badly ravaged by storm and time. In 1916 while the lettering was still legible it was recorded as:—

CNEGUMI FILI (son of) GENAIUS

The stone is estimated to be at least 1500 years old and with the inscription in Latin might well have been a memorial to a Roman at the time of their occupation.

The Seal Sanctuary

We are now on the last part of our journey in the higher reaches of the river toward Gweek where on the Northern bank a Seal Sanctuary operates. Injured seals have always been washed in around the Cornish coast but now under the promotion and tender care of its curator Ken Jones, these are looked after by experts. These baby seals aged anything from one day to six weeks get washed in usually between September and March often having been parted from their mothers through severe gales. Some have serious injuries, others are desperately weak through starvation. Pollution and storm are mainly responsible for their condition. Some lose eyes, some break jaws, others have damaged flippers or bad lung condition. The healthy ones are returned to the sea as quickly as possible but where their condition is such that it would be cruel to do so, others are kept in the sanctuary or sold to Wild Life parks.

Open to the public, the Sanctuary depends on entrance fees from tourists to cope with running expenses.

Gweek

And so to Gweek with its two granite stone bridges astride the narrowing waterway carrying the main road, running North to Penryn and West to Helston.

At the moment, the quays are crowded with small craft under various stages of repair and maintenance in these boat-yards, for hereabouts the river is so badly silted up that only craft with shallow draughts can reach Gweek. At one time it was an important centre of trade in the days when Cornish Mining flourished and roads were fit only for horses, for in the nearby valleys tin mining and streaming was a thriving industry with the tracks resounding to the clatter of pack-horses carrying ore to the blowing houses at Gweek. At the time when the river was less silted up and larger craft could reach the old quays, barges brought cargoes of timber props for the mines. These were off-loaded on to strong drays and hauled by huge shire-horses along the rutted and pitted roads.

The port itself lies in three parishes, Mawgan, Wendron and Constantine. In early times, the port was shared by the lords of Merthen and Helston. It is recorded that in the year 1301 Roger de Carmenou was asked to show his warrant for having a gallows at 'Wyke'. At the same time, the Burgesses of Helston were confirmed in their own right to use Gweek as their port, to hang their own thieves at the gallows at 'Wyke' and to decide any disputes arising in the said water between merchants and seamen. The situation of 'Wyke' in the Middle Ages, being in the heart of the country and protected from storms and hostile attack by a long winding estuary, made it a valuable port.

The tide is on the ebb; if we stay longer we could find ourselves stranded on the mud banks with little chance of being rescued for several hours, but the scene is exceedingly beautiful, with the trees from deeply wooded banks suspended over the still water reflecting every branch as in a mirror. Families of swans, brilliantly white against the green black river, raise their proud heads inquiringly as we drift by. A curlew's cry echoes across the glassy waters of the quiet creek and nearby the gentle plop of a leaping fish, as it seizes the unsuspecting fly for which it ever seeks.

This is the Helford, a haven of peace and tranquility, complacently beautiful in its serenity and contentedly ignorant of the march of progress.